ESSENTIAL
AMPHIBIANS

by Marie Pearson

CONTENT CONSULTANT

Brian I. Crother, PhD
Edward G. Schlieder Foundation Professor
Department of Biological Sciences
Southeastern Louisiana University

ESSENTIAL
ANIMALS

Essential Library
An Imprint of Abdo Publishing
abdobooks.com

abdobooks.com

Published by Abdo Publishing, a division of ABDO, PO Box 398166, Minneapolis, Minnesota 55439. Copyright © 2022 by Abdo Consulting Group, Inc. International copyrights reserved in all countries. No part of this book may be reproduced in any form without written permission from the publisher. Essential Library™ is a trademark and logo of Abdo Publishing.

Printed in the United States of America, North Mankato, Minnesota.
102021
012022

THIS BOOK CONTAINS RECYCLED MATERIALS

Cover Photos: Chris Ison/Shutterstock Images, (cane toad); Michiel de Wit/Shutterstock Images, (American toad); Shutterstock Images, (tree frog); Eric Isselee/Shutterstock Images, (axolotl), (fire-bellied toad); Marco Maggesi/Shutterstock Images, (salamander)

Interior Photos: Shutterstock Images, 1, 6, 25 (bed) 38–39, 45, 65, 66, 83, 92, 93, 97, 102 (axolotl), 103 (tomato frog), 103 (flying frog); Eugene Kuryashov/Shutterstock Images, 4; Dirk Ercken/Shutterstock Images, 5, 69 (right), 70–71; Manuel Findeis/Shutterstock Images, 7 (left); Milan Zygmunt/Shutterstock Images, 7 (middle), 39; Fabio Maffei/Shutterstock Images, 7 (right); Federico Crovetto/Shutterstock Images, 9, 37; Elena Yakimova/Shutterstock Images, 10; Eric Isselee/Shutterstock Images, 11, 69 (left), 78, 103 (fire-bellied toad); David Byron Keener/Shutterstock Images, 12, 102 (bullfrog); Christian Ouellet/Shutterstock Images, 13; ER Degginger/Science Source, 14 (top left), 14 (bottom left), 29, 102 (mudpuppy); Ivan Kuzmin/Science Source, 14 (top right); Amy Lutz/Shutterstock Images, 14 (bottom right); Frode Jacobsen/Shutterstock Images, 16, 17, 102 (American toad); Michael Benard/Shutterstock Images, 19, 32, 33, 58; Randy Bjorklund/Shutterstock Images, 20, 103 (cane toad); Arlan Carletto/Shutterstock Images, 21; Trevor Charles Graham/Shutterstock Images, 23; Tristan Tan/Shutterstock Images, 24, 103 (giant salamander); Red Line Editorial, 25 (salamander), 102–103; Eliza Remark/Shutterstock Images, 25 (guitar); Goh Chai Hin/AFP/Getty Images, 26; Gary Meszaros/Science Source, 28; Ted Kinsman/Science Source, 30–31; Liz Weber/Shutterstock Images, 34, 102 (eastern newt); Wild Media/Shutterstock Images, 36, 103 (fire salamander); Alex Hyde/NaturePL/Science Source, 40; Gregory G. Dimijian/Science Source, 41; Dr. Morley Read/Science Source, 42, 102 (glass frog); Thorsten Spoerlein/Shutterstock Images, 44, 46, 47, 102 (golden poison frog); Dr. Paul A. Zahl/Science Source, 48; Daniel Heuclin/Biosphoto/Science Source, 49, 103 (goliath frog); Cyril Ruoso/Biosphoto/Alamy, 50; Jay Ondreicka/Shutterstock Images, 52, 102 (hellbender); Nature and Science/Alamy, 53; Phil A. Dotson/Science Source, 54; Mike Wilhelm/Shutterstock Images, 56, 102 (Jefferson salamander); Tom McHugh/Science Source, 57, 91; Suzanne L. and Joseph T. Collins/Science Source, 60, 102 (lesser siren); Barry Blackburn/Shutterstock Images, 61; iStockphoto, 62–63, 88, 89, 102 (rough-skinned newt); Vitaliy Halenov/iStockphoto, 64; Frank Cornelissen/Shutterstock Images, 68, 102 (mimic poison frog); Luca Cavallari/Shutterstock Images, 72, 103 (olm); Francesco Tomasinelli/Science Source, 73; Philippe Psaila/Science Source, 74; Kirsanov Valeriy Vladimirovich/Shutterstock Images, 76; Kurit Afshen/Shutterstock Images, 77; David Havel/Shutterstock Images, 80, 102 (tree frog); Sascha Burkard/Shutterstock Images, 81; Dave Denby Photography/Shutterstock Images, 82; Danté Fenolio/Science Source, 84, 85, 102 (caecilian); Chris Mattison/Alamy, 86; Lubo Ivanko/Shutterstock Images, 94; Valt Ahyppo/Shutterstock Images, 95; Stephen Dalton/Science Source, 96; Arif Supriyadi/Shutterstock Images, 98–99

Editor: Katharine Hale
Series Designer: Sarah Taplin

Library of Congress Control Number: 2020949097

Publisher's Cataloging-in-Publication Data

Names: Pearson, Marie, author.
Title: Essential amphibians / by Marie Pearson
Description: Minneapolis, Minnesota : Abdo Publishing, 2022 | Series: Essential animals | Includes online resources and index.
Identifiers: ISBN 9781532195501 (lib. bdg.) | ISBN 9781098215880 (ebook)
Subjects: LCSH: Amphibians--Juvenile literature. | Amphibians--Behavior--Juvenile literature. | Animals--Identification--Juvenile literature. | Zoology--Juvenile literature.
Classification: DDC 597.8--dc23

CONTENTS

| INTRODUCTION | 4 |

AMERICAN BULLFROG	12
AMERICAN TOAD	16
CANE TOAD	20
CHINESE GIANT SALAMANDER	24
COMMON MUDPUPPY	28
EASTERN NEWT	32
FIRE SALAMANDER	36
FLEISCHMANN'S GLASS FROG	40
GOLDEN POISON FROG	44
GOLIATH FROG	48
HELLBENDER	52
JEFFERSON SALAMANDER	56
LESSER SIREN	60
MEXICAN AXOLOTL	64
MIMIC POISON FROG	68
OLM	72
ORIENTAL FIRE-BELLIED TOAD	76
RED-EYED TREE FROG	80
RINGED CAECILIAN	84
ROUGH-SKINNED NEWT	88
TOMATO FROG	92
WALLACE'S FLYING FROG	96

ESSENTIAL FACTS	100
AMPHIBIANS AROUND THE WORLD	102
GLOSSARY	104
ADDITIONAL RESOURCES	106
SOURCE NOTES	108
INDEX	110
ABOUT THE AUTHOR	112
ABOUT THE CONSULTANT	112

INTRODUCTION

Scientists can study amphibians to learn about ecosystem health.

Some people find amphibians too slimy to appreciate, but these animals are very important. They are especially important for scientists, who study amphibians to monitor the health of habitats. Amphibians are sensitive to their environments. Their skins easily absorb substances, including toxins. Because many spend part of their time on land and part in water, they are exposed to toxins in both places. When toxins enter an amphibian, these substances build up. This can lead to health problems and death.

Scientists can track the number of amphibians in an area. If the number starts to drop, something may be wrong in the habitat. Scientists can study the habitat further. There may be toxic chemicals or an invasive species. Once scientists know what is wrong, they can figure out ways to make the habitat healthy again. Amphibians can be the key to restoring a healthy ecosystem.

CLASSIFYING AMPHIBIANS

Amphibians belong to the class Amphibia. Class is one of the major levels of scientific classification. Scientists use classification to group living things based on how closely they are related to one another. From broadest to most specific, the levels of classification are kingdom, phylum, class, order, family, genus, and species. All animals belong to the kingdom Animalia. Amphibians are part of the phylum Chordata. All animals in this phylum have a notochord at some point in their lives. The notochord develops into the backbone in many animals, including amphibians.

The class Amphibia is divided into three orders. Those orders are Anura, Caudata, and Gymnophiona. Each order contains many individual species. Species typically have both common names and scientific names. For example, most people

Frogs belong to the order Anura.

INTRODUCTION

use the common name *goliath frog* to refer to the largest frog species. However, sometimes two different species may be called by the same common name. Or the common name for an animal may not be the same in different languages. Experts use scientific names to clearly distinguish different animals. The scientific name is unique to that species and is the same around the world. It is made up of the genus and the species. For example, the goliath frog is known scientifically as *Conraua goliath*.

Anura is the order of frogs and toads. It is the most diverse order of amphibians. These animals typically have broad, flat heads. Their bodies are short, and they do not have tails. Their hind legs are long and strong, allowing them to leap. Most have specialized features that allow them to either dig into the ground or climb trees. They rely primarily on their excellent vision to hunt. While people may speak of frogs and toads as distinct types of animals, toads are actually frogs. The term *toad* is generally used for frogs in the family Bufonidae.

The order Caudata contains salamanders and newts. These animals have long bodies and tails. Their heads are relatively small. Most salamanders have smooth skin

AMPHIBIAN EXTREMES

There is a lot of diversity in the amphibian class. Some amphibians are as long as an adult human is tall. The Chinese giant salamander is the largest amphibian. It grows up to 5.9 feet (1.8 m) long from nose to tail. It can weigh 25 pounds (11 kg). The smallest known amphibian does not have a common name. Its scientific name is *Paedophryne amauensis*. This frog is just 0.3 inches (0.7 cm) long.[1] That is approximately half the diameter of a dime. This frog is also the smallest known vertebrate.

and live mainly on land as adults. The term *newt* is used for certain salamanders with rough skin that typically live in the water as adults.

The third order, Gymnophiona, contains caecilians. These worm-like animals live underground. Their heads are small and bony to help them tunnel. They do not have limbs, and they have poor eyesight. Their eyes are typically covered by a layer of skin or even bone. Scientists think they may only be able to distinguish between light and dark.

AMPHIBIAN ORDERS

FROGS (ANURA)
Broad, flat head
Short body
No tail
Long, strong legs for leaping

SALAMANDERS (CAUDATA)
Long body
Long tail
Small head
Short legs

CAECILIANS (GYMNOPHIONA)
Small, bony head
Long body
No limbs

INTRODUCTION

Amphibians live on every continent except Antarctica. They are also absent from a few particularly dry deserts and very remote islands. Most live in warm climates, though some live just above the Arctic Circle. Caecilians only live in tropical zones. In general, amphibians need moist habitats. Most spend part of their lives in water and part on land. But a few live either entirely in the water or entirely on land.

SLIPPERY AND SLIMY

There are very few features that all amphibians share. The main trait shared among them is the inability to internally control body temperature. An amphibian uses its surroundings to regulate its body temperature. If it is too warm, it may seek water or a cool hole in the ground. If it is cold, it will look for a patch of sunlight.

The skin of most amphibians easily absorbs substances. This aids in breathing by absorbing oxygen. Some amphibians don't have lungs at all and rely only on their skins to breathe. Because amphibians lose a lot of water through their skins, they need easy access to moisture. Many have mucus coating their skins. This mucus helps them stay moist and assists in breathing. Amphibian skin also typically has toxins used for defense. The bad taste of these toxins can prevent predators from eating amphibians, and sometimes it even poisons predators.

Most amphibians go through metamorphosis. They change forms as they grow up. Most species lay eggs. The larvae that

FUN FACT

Frogs in colder climates may freeze in the winter. Their hearts and brain activity completely stop. Then they thaw in warmer weather.

INTRODUCTION

Most amphibians lay eggs.

hatch typically live fully in the water. They have tails with fins to help them swim. They also have gills. Typically the larvae do not look like the adults. As they grow, they begin to change into their adult forms. They may absorb their gills and develop lungs. They lose the fins on their tails or lose their tails entirely. They usually move from water to land. Frogs and toads exhibit the most dramatic change from larval to adult form.

However, all three orders have some species that undergo direct development. This means that the young develop in the egg and hatch with the same body structures as adults. A few species of amphibians give birth to live young.

IMPORTANCE

Amphibians are predators. They eat worms, insects, and small birds and mammals. They help control the populations of insect pests that damage crops. They also eat mosquitoes,

INTRODUCTION

which can carry diseases that can spread to humans. Amphibians are also prey, providing an important food source to snakes and large birds. Scientists study amphibian skin secretions for possible medical uses. Some secretions can be used to make antibiotics, anesthetics, or painkillers.

Amphibian populations around the world are shrinking. Poor water quality, diseases, climate change, invasive species, and habitat loss from human development are all contributing to this decline. One of the most serious threats is the chytrid fungus. Scientists first documented the fungus in the 1990s. It damages an amphibian's skin, which makes it difficult for the amphibian to breathe. The chytrid fungus has led to the death of many amphibians, and it has even caused some species to go extinct.

ESSENTIAL AMPHIBIANS

This book presents 22 notable amphibian species from around the world. The species are presented alphabetically by their common names. These amphibians represent the amazing diversity of appearance and behavior in the class Amphibia. They range in size from the small golden poison frog to the enormous Chinese giant salamander. Some, such as the American bullfrog, are short and stocky. Others, such as the ringed caecilian, are long and thin. Each species plays an important role in its ecosystem. Narrative stories, colorful photos, fact boxes, and the latest scientific findings help bring these slimy creatures to life.

AMERICAN BULLFROG

The American bullfrog is native to North America.

The female American bullfrog enters the water at the edge of a pond in Florida. Surrounded by cattails, she begins laying 20,000 eggs on the water's surface.[2] Then she leaves. Just four days later, tadpoles hatch from the eggs. The tadpoles are greenish yellow. Dark spots speckle their backs. Each tadpole has a round body with a long tail. It uses gills to breathe underwater. Occasionally a tadpole comes up to the surface to gulp air using its lungs. The tadpoles swim into the deeper water of the pond, eating aquatic plants. The fish in the pond do not eat the tadpoles because they taste bad.

Within a few months, the tadpoles are swimming closer to shore. They begin transforming. They lose their gills and tails and grow legs. Soon, they leave the pond to hop around on the ground. Their metamorphosis is complete. They are now adult frogs.

APPEARANCE AND BEHAVIOR

The adult American bullfrog is the largest frog in North America. Its skin is brown to green with darker splotches on the back. It has long, powerful hind legs, and its back feet are webbed to help with swimming. The bullfrog's front legs are shorter, and the front feet are not webbed.

Male bullfrogs look a bit different from females. Males are smaller and have yellow throats. Behind either eye of the bullfrog sits a large, round eardrum. The male's eardrum is twice the width of its eye. In the female, the eardrum is the same size as the eye.

Tadpoles eat aquatic plants, but adult bullfrogs are predators. They feed on insects, snakes, small fish and birds, and amphibians, including other bullfrogs. An adult bullfrog sits and waits for prey to pass by. Then it flicks out its sticky tongue to capture the animal. It can also leap to catch an animal in its mouth.

Bullfrogs breed from spring into early summer. Each male defends a breeding area in the shallows of a body of water. A male sits in his territory and calls out to females. His call is a deep drone that some people think sounds like a cow mooing. Females tend to select older, larger mates. The females become pickier as they age. Tadpoles stay in the larval stage for a few months in southern parts of North America and up to three years in the northern regions.[3] Cold temperatures limit a tadpole's growth.

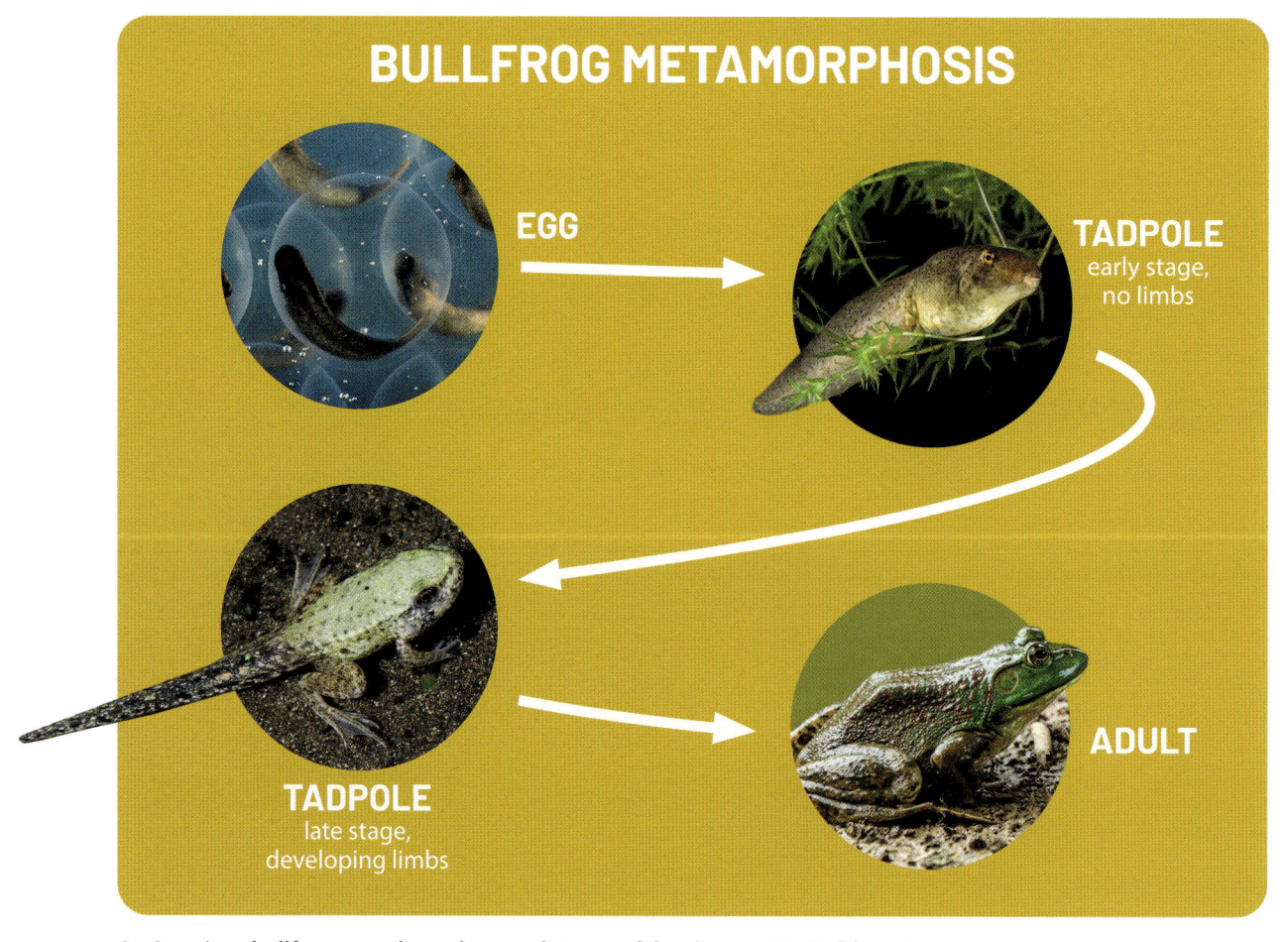

BULLFROG METAMORPHOSIS

EGG → TADPOLE (early stage, no limbs) → TADPOLE (late stage, developing limbs) → ADULT

An American bullfrog goes through several stages of development in its life cycle.

In places with cold winters, bullfrogs hibernate underwater. They dig into the mud and wait for warmer temperatures to return.

INVADING THE WORLD

American bullfrogs are highly invasive. While they naturally exist across much of North America, they were only recently introduced to the West Coast, including California. Because they eat many kinds of food, they contribute to population losses of native amphibians by both directly preying on those amphibians and by competing with them for food resources. In addition, while American bullfrogs are not much affected by the chytrid fungus, they can spread it to other amphibians. American bullfrogs introduced to Europe, Asia, and South America have caused similar issues.

FUN FACT

Bullfrogs' powerful hind legs make them excellent jumpers. Some people catch bullfrogs and enter them in races.

AMERICAN BULLFROG
Lithobates catesbeianus

SIZE
3.7–4.9 inches (9.5–12.5 cm) from nose to ischium

WEIGHT
Up to 1.1 pounds (0.5 kg)

RANGE
Native to North America; invasive in Europe, South America, Asia

HABITAT
Areas near water, including bogs, lakes, ponds, rivers

DIET
Any animal smaller than itself, including other frogs, insects, crayfish, mice, snails, small fish and birds, snakes

LIFE SPAN
8–10 years in the wild; up to 16 years in captivity

AMERICAN TOAD

Male American toads are smaller than females. A male toad will ride on a female's back while she searches for a place to lay her eggs.

The young American toad sits in the grass. It has grown over the last couple of weeks and is ready to shed its skin. It bites at some loose skin on its front leg and pulls. The moist layer of skin peels away from the layer beneath it. The toad gives another tug at the skin, using its tongue to pull the strip farther into its mouth. After one final tug, the shed skin separates from the toad's toes. The amphibian snaps up the last strands of skin and gulps them down. Its body can use the skin as food, getting nutrients from it. The toad will repeat this shedding process until it is fully grown. From then on, it will shed its skin four times a year.[4]

WARTS AND ALL

An adult American toad has a stocky body. Its skin is typically brown and covered in red and yellow bumps called warts. Females are larger than males. Males have dark-brown or black throats, while females have white throats.

Males join together in spring and early summer to call for females. They trill together, and females seek a large male with a desirable call. However, other males may try to stop females as they seek out the right male.

Females lay their eggs in still, shallow ponds. Tadpoles hatch from the eggs and live in the pond for approximately two months, when they develop their adult bodies.[5]

PREDATORS AND PREDATION

American toads spend the day under rocks, logs, or other shelters. They may also dig into the soil. Adults hunt many kinds of insects and other invertebrates. When one of these toads finds a meal, it shoots out its sticky tongue to catch the creature. If the insect is large, the toad will shove the insect into its mouth with its front feet. The American toad helps control many species of insect pests.

Snakes are the main predators of American toads. If a toad senses danger, it will freeze. Its coloring can make it look like a pile of dirt, and a predator may not notice it. The toad will also take a deep breath, making its body larger and more difficult to swallow. In addition, glands on the toad's skin produce a poison that repels some animals. However, some predators are immune to the poison.

FUN FACT

An American toad can eat as many as 1,000 insects in just a single day.[6]

Female toads typically lay eggs in ponds without fish. But the eggs are further protected with camouflage. The tops of the eggs are dark. This allows them to blend in with the water when viewed from above. The bottoms of the eggs are light. They blend in with the sky when seen from below.

When calling to females, a male American toad's throat puffs up.

AMERICAN TOAD
Anaxyrus americanus

SIZE
2–4 inches (5–10 cm) from nose to ischium

WEIGHT
Approximately 1.8–3.9 ounces (50–110 g)

RANGE
North America

HABITAT
Semipermanent freshwater ponds or pools; areas with dense vegetation on land

DIET
Tadpoles eat aquatic plants and algae; adults eat insects and other invertebrates

LIFE SPAN
1–2 years in the wild; longer in captivity

CANE TOAD

The cane toad is considered one of the most damaging invasive species in the world.

It is evening in Brazil's Amazon rain forest. A cane toad hops near a stream at the edge of a town. A dog passing by sees the motion and chases after it. The dog grabs the toad and takes a bite. It isn't really hungry, so it doesn't continue eating. But soon, the dog starts staggering, panting, and drooling. It collapses and begins seizing. Its body goes stiff. Within 15 minutes, the dog is dead.

Poison from the cane toad's skin killed the dog. A cane toad has glands on the back of its neck that produce the poison. A predator that eats the toad can become very sick or die if it is not immune to the toxin. Eliminating predators protects other cane toads from being eaten in the future.

APPEARANCE AND REPRODUCTION

Adult cane toads are large, brown toads. Their warty skins can be mottled shades of light and dark brown. A ridge runs from above each eye and down the nose. A large poison-producing gland sits behind each eye and runs down the side of the body toward the front leg. Most commonly, poison is absorbed into the predator's bloodstream through the mouth when it tries to eat the toad. The poison can irritate human skin. If someone has a cut, it can enter the bloodstream there. Once absorbed, the poison can be dangerous or even fatal.

When males are ready to mate, they gather in calm water and call for females. When a female has selected a

> **FUN FACT**
> Cane toad poison is strong enough to kill a crocodile. The toads have been linked to population declines of freshwater and dwarf crocodiles in Australia.

male, the male climbs onto her back and holds on with his front legs. He may ride on her back for several days while she travels and feeds. Then she lays her eggs in jelly strings, attaching them to rocks or vegetation in the water. She can lay up to 20,000 eggs at once.[7]

Tadpoles hatch from the eggs after just two or three days. Their backs are black, and their silver-white bellies have black spots. Like the adults, they are poisonous. The tadpoles feed on algae in the water. If there are older tadpoles in the water already, the younger tadpoles need to be careful. Older tadpoles, immune to the poison, will sometimes eat younger ones. In approximately 45 days, the tadpoles will have transformed into their adult bodies.[8] Then they will move to land and hunt insects.

INVASIVE TOADS

Humans introduced cane toads to Australia in 1935 to control cane beetles, which were eating sugarcane crops. But instead of controlling the beetle population, the cane toad population also grew out of control. Cane toad predators in the toad's native range have developed a tolerance to the toad's poison. But much of Australia's wildlife lacks a tolerance to this poison. As a result, Australia's predator populations have declined. A few species, including some birds, have learned to slice open the frogs and only eat the insides, avoiding the poisonous skin. But many species remain vulnerable.

Having few predators in Australia is just one reason for the toad's success. They do not need a large amount of water, so they can survive in many habitats. In addition, they can eat many kinds of animals, so they are not often without food. Cane toads sometimes eat native amphibians, and they also compete with those native species for food. While people are attempting to control cane toad populations in Australia, these amphibians are likely there to stay.

The Australian keelback snake is one of only a few native predators that can eat the invasive cane toad.

CANE TOAD
Rhinella marina

SIZE
4–6 inches (10–15 cm) long

WEIGHT
3.7 ounces (106 g) on average

RANGE
Native from the Rio Grande Valley of Texas down to the Amazon rain forest and southeastern Peru; invasive in Australia, Florida, Hawaii, Caribbean islands

HABITAT
Places with semipermanent water and forests nearby

DIET
Tadpoles eat algae; adults eat amphibians, insects, spiders, crabs, other invertebrates

LIFE SPAN
10 years in the wild; 15 years in captivity

CHINESE GIANT SALAMANDER

The Chinese giant salamander can grow up to 5.9 feet (1.8 m) long.

A team of researchers gathers at nightfall along a cold, rushing mountain stream in China. Members pull on their wet suits and wade into the water. Using headlamps to see, they lift tent-shaped traps from the water to check for the largest amphibian on Earth: the Chinese giant salamander.[9]

They've found one. The researchers rub cotton swabs along the feet and inside the mouth of the long, dark-brown animal. The swabs will be tested for diseases and used to collect information about the salamander's genetics. This species is critically endangered as a result of poachers hunting them for meat. The information the researchers gather will help them protect the Chinese giant salamander.

APPEARANCE AND HUNTING

The Chinese giant salamander's rough skin is dark brown, green, or black. The salamander has a long body with a flat, wide head. Its small, lidless eyes have poor vision, and its mouth is large. The salamander's four legs are short, and its tail is broad and flattened. A dorsal fin

HOW LONG IS A CHINESE GIANT SALAMANDER?

CHINESE GIANT SALAMANDER
3.3 feet (1 m)

FULL-SIZED GUITAR
3.3 feet (1 m)

TWIN BED
6.3 feet (1.9 m)

Chinese giant salamanders grow to 3.3 feet (1 m) long on average. See how they measure up to common household objects.

runs from the lower back down the tail. Adults do not have gills. They use lungs to breathe air when on land. But most of the time they are underwater. They absorb oxygen through their skins.

These salamanders are top predators in their habitats. At night they hunt fish, other amphibians, worms, crabs, and more. Sometimes they even eat other Chinese giant salamanders. The salamanders rely on sensory nodes along their sides to detect motion in the water. When they've found food, they suck it up with their mouths.

REPRODUCTION

In August, a male salamander finds an underwater cave or cavity. He cleans the cave, clearing any sand or gravel by pushing it out of the hole. After several days, the den has a

Except for their smaller size and gills, baby Chinese giant salamanders resemble adults.

smooth bottom. Females select males partially based on the cleanliness of the den. Once a female has selected a male, she lays a few hundred eggs in the den. Then the male sprays the eggs with sperm to fertilize them.

After laying the eggs, the female leaves. The male stays to guard the eggs from predators. The male fans the eggs with his tail, stirring up the water to bring oxygen to the eggs. He eats any unfertilized eggs or eggs that have gotten moldy to keep bacteria from spreading to the other eggs.

When the larvae hatch a month or two later, they are on their own. The larvae look similar to the adults. But they differ from adults in that they have gills. Lungs begin to develop approximately eight months later. By the time the salamanders are 2.5 to three years old, they have lost their gills and have their adult bodies.[10]

FUN FACT

Male Chinese giant salamanders are called den masters because of how they clean and defend their dens and eggs.

CHINESE GIANT SALAMANDER
Andrias davidianus

SIZE
3.3 feet (1 m) long on average, up to 5.9 feet (1.8 m) long

WEIGHT
24 pounds (11 kg) on average

RANGE
China

HABITAT
Mountain streams, sometimes lakes

DIET
Fish, other amphibians, worms, crabs, other invertebrates

LIFE SPAN
60 years on average in the wild and captivity

COMMON MUDPUPPY

Common mudpuppies eat crayfish and other aquatic organisms.

A common mudpuppy crawls along the rocky bottom of a cold river in Michigan. Short legs propel its long body, which snakes around the rocks as the salamander searches for food. On either side of its head, red, feathery external gills ripple with the water. The mudpuppy uses its sense of smell to find worms, crayfish, and other food.

Suddenly sensory organs in the mudpuppy's skin detect motion in the water. The mudpuppy darts under a rock just as a large fish torpedoes over and snaps at where the salamander floated just a moment ago. The mudpuppy has escaped.

AQUATIC SALAMANDER

The common mudpuppy lives its life underwater. It has gray, brown, or nearly black skin with dark spots. The belly is lighter. Its head is flat, and its small eyes see mainly light. Its tail is shorter than its body and somewhat vertically flattened like the tail of a fish. While it usually walks along the floors of bodies of water, the mudpuppy can swim with the side-to-side movement of a fish. The mudpuppy retains some larval traits into adulthood, including its gills. Although an adult mudpuppy does have lungs and can gulp air, it primarily breathes with its gills.

Mudpuppies live from southeastern Canada to the southeastern United States. Temperatures in some of these places can

FUN FACT

Mudpuppies have very slimy skin, which can make them difficult to hold. They may bite, though they are not venomous.

get very cold, and ice may form on the water's surface. But mudpuppies stay active all year. They move to deep water in the winter, where the temperatures are warmer.

GROWING UP

Each female lays approximately 60 eggs in a nest under a log or other shelter.[11] She guards the nest for one or two months until the larvae hatch. The larvae are black and have a cream or yellow stripe running down both sides of the back.

Larvae are on their own. They find shelter during the day under rocks and other objects. Nighttime is typically when they forage for food. Mudpuppies aren't able to reproduce until they are four to six years old.[12]

Mudpuppies have many predators, including fish, birds, snakes, otters, and other salamanders. They use their quick swimming ability to escape from predators. They press their legs tight against their bodies and wriggle their bodies and tails from side to side.

COMMON MUDPUPPY
Necturus maculosus

SIZE
0.7–1.1 feet (20–33 cm) from nose to tail

WEIGHT
Unavailable

RANGE
From southeastern Canada to the southeastern United States

HABITAT
Canals, ditches, lakes, reservoirs, streams; must have shelter such as logs or weeds

DIET
Aquatic organisms, including crayfish, insect larvae, small fish, worms, snails, other amphibians

LIFE SPAN
11 years on average in the wild; 20 years on average in captivity

EASTERN NEWT

The eastern newt's appearance changes dramatically from larva, *pictured*, to eft, to adult.

A jelly-covered egg clings to an underwater plant in a forest pond. An eastern newt larva hatches from the egg. The larva is olive colored, with feathery gills and a long, finned tail. Its legs are small and not well developed. The larva lives in the pond for five months. By this time it has matured into an eft. In this stage, the newt leaves the pond and travels on land. Orange-red skin covers its body. The eft breathes air with its lungs, and its legs are longer and stronger. It has no tail fin. The eft crawls slowly across fallen leaves. Its body bends left and right as it walks.

After living as an eft on land for three years, the animal transforms once more. The newt matures into its larger adult body. The skin becomes greenish brown with red spots. The tail develops a fin again. The eastern newt returns to the water, where it lives out the rest of its life.

HABITAT AND SUBSPECIES

Eastern newts are mostly aquatic, spending their time as larvae and adults in the water. However, if an adult's pond or other aquatic home dries up, it can live on land. Some eastern newts move straight from the larval to adult stages. But most have an in-between stage as an eft. Efts live on land, hiding under fallen leaves and in other moist areas.

FUN FACT

Some people keep eastern newts as pets in aquariums. Up to three adults can live together in a 10-gallon (40 L) tank.

Adult eastern newts return to an aquatic lifestyle.

EASTERN NEWT

Males and females look similar, except during the breeding season in late winter and early spring. Then males' legs become thicker and develop black, horn-like growths on the insides of their thighs and on their toes. There are four subspecies, and they differ slightly in appearance. The red-spotted newt has red spots edged in black. It lives in eastern Canada and the United States. The central newt typically does not have red spots, or it may have

An eft's bright coloring warns predators of its poison.

red spots that are not fully encircled with black. This newt lives in the central and southern United States. The broken-striped newt has red stripes, rather than spots, edged in black. It lives in the Carolina coastal plains. Finally, the peninsula newt has black spots. It lives on the Florida peninsula.

LIFE AS A NEWT

Eastern newts at all stages face predators, including amphibians, birds, fish, and mammals. Larvae rarely survive into adulthood. Adult newts sometimes eat the larvae. Once newts enter the eft stage, they develop poison glands, which deter many predators. In addition to having poisonous secretions, adult eastern newts are excellent swimmers. Their finned tails help them swim quickly. Because of their short legs, they walk slowly on land.

Some eastern newts live in deep bodies of water that do not freeze all the way through during the coldest parts of the year. These newts remain active underwater all winter. Newts that live in bodies of water that dry up or completely freeze in the winter burrow underground instead.

EASTERN NEWT
Notophthalmus viridescens

SIZE
2.8–4.9 inches (7–12.4 cm) long from nose to tail

WEIGHT
Unavailable

RANGE
Eastern Canada, United States

HABITAT
Forests with small bodies of fresh water

DIET
Larvae and adults eat small invertebrates in the water; efts eat small invertebrates on the ground

LIFE SPAN
12–15 years in the wild and captivity

FIRE SALAMANDER

The fire salamander is found in Europe, northern Africa, and the Middle East.

It is daytime in a forest in Germany. The fire salamander hides in the moist soil under a rock. This keeps the sunlight from drying out its black-and-yellow skin. Then the clouds begin rolling in. Rain is coming. The fire salamander leaves its shelter to hunt.

The rain arrives, and soon worms have surfaced on the forest floor. A leaf nearby twitches. A worm is inching along beside the leaf. The salamander crawls toward it, pauses, then snaps up the worm with its jaws. There will be plenty of worms for the salamander to eat today.

APPEARANCE AND BEHAVIOR

Fire salamanders are black with orange or yellow spots or bands. The belly is black or brown. The tail is round and a bit shorter than the length of the body. Females are slightly larger than males.

Eggs develop inside the female fire salamander. Then she gives birth to live young in shallow water. Some subspecies of fire salamanders give birth to young that already have adult-shaped bodies. Other subspecies give birth to larvae. The larvae have external gills and tail fins. They go through metamorphosis a few months later.

Adults live on land and are mostly active at twilight. Those that live in colder habitats hibernate in the winter, while those that live in warm places become inactive during the hot summer. Fire salamanders typically hibernate in groups, and they may use the same cave for hibernation many years in a row.

FUN FACT
People once thought fire salamanders could live in fire, but they can't. This belief likely came from seeing them crawl from logs used in campfires.

FIRE SALAMANDER

THREATS

The fire salamander is not in danger of extinction, but its numbers are declining. These salamanders are popular pets and are sometimes taken from the wild. Laws make it illegal to take salamanders from the wild. This helps to protect their populations.

Fire salamander habitats are shrinking because of deforestation. Habitats are broken up by cities, roads, and other human development. A type of chytrid fungus is another major threat to these salamanders. In the early 2010s, nearly half of all captive fire salamanders died.[13] Researchers discovered they had been infected with a type of chytrid fungus.

Infected salamanders lost their appetites and lost their coordination when they moved. They died within days of infection. Wild populations are affected too. While the fungus that affects frogs hardens the skin, the variety affecting salamanders causes ulcers to form on the skin. Researchers worry that the fungus could eventually lead to the salamander's extinction in Europe. Scientists are looking for ways to help protect the fire salamander and other European salamanders from this threat.

Fire salamanders face human-made threats such as deforestation as well as natural threats such as chytrid fungus.

FIRE SALAMANDER
Salamandra salamandra

SIZE
5.9–11.8 inches (15–30 cm) long from nose to tail, on average

WEIGHT
0.67 ounces (19 g) on average

RANGE
Central and southern Europe into northern Africa and the Middle East

HABITAT
Forests, especially those with shade, ponds, streams

DIET
Invertebrates including worms, slugs, flies, millipedes, beetles

LIFE SPAN
10 years on average in the wild; 24 years on average in captivity

FLEISCHMANN'S GLASS FROG

A Fleischmann's glass frog parent protects its eggs from predators.

A female Fleischmann's glass frog lays 20 eggs on a leaf.[14] The leaf hangs over a stream in a Central American forest. At night, the male and female both sit on the eggs. During the day, the parents sleep near the eggs, ready to protect them from predators. The male eats damaged eggs to keep them from spreading disease to the others. Occasionally when he sits on the eggs, he urinates on them to keep them moist. After ten days, the tadpoles hatch and drop into the stream below, where they will continue to develop.[15] The parents' job is done.

FLEISCHMANN'S GLASS FROG

SEE-THROUGH SKIN

Fleischmann's glass frogs are one of many species of glass frog. A lot of glass frogs, including the Fleischmann's glass frog, have transparent skin on the abdomen. This trait inspired their common name. Their internal organs are visible through the skin. The covering surrounding the lungs, heart, and liver is visible in the Fleischmann's glass frog. Blood vessels are also visible.

This frog's golden eyes point forward, and its snout is short. The skin on its back is pale green and

FUN FACT

Parental care among frogs, such as caring for eggs, is rare. Scientists estimate that only 10 to 20 percent of frog species care for their young.[16]

41

FLEISCHMANN'S GLASS FROG

Fleischmann's glass frogs use vocal calls for mating rituals and establishing territory.

covered with yellow or yellow-green spots. Its toes are yellow. Females are a bit larger than males. Males have a bony structure growing from each upper arm. Scientists believe the frogs may use these structures to defend their territories from other frogs.

BEHAVIOR

There is still a lot to be learned about the Fleischmann's glass frog. But scientists do know some things about this frog's behavior. This glass frog spends its life in the trees and is mostly active at night. Its mating season is long, lasting from March into November. Males attract females by making a short peeping sound. They often hang upside down on leaves while calling.

As much as 80 percent of the eggs from each pair of glass frogs do not hatch.[17] Some end up with fungal infections, and others are eaten by parasites. Some flies lay their eggs alongside the frog eggs. When the fly larvae hatch, they eat many of the frog eggs. A tadpole that does hatch will live in the water for one or two years before completing metamorphosis.[18]

FLEISCHMANN'S GLASS FROG
Hyalinobatrachium fleischmanni

SIZE
0.9–1 inch (2.2–2.5 cm) long from nose to vent, on average

WEIGHT
0.03–0.05 ounces (0.9–1.4 g)

RANGE
Mexico, Central America, South America

HABITAT
Humid, mountainous forests

DIET
Likely small invertebrates

LIFE SPAN
Unavailable

GOLDEN POISON FROG

Golden poison frogs are the most poisonous frogs in the world.

Researchers and conservationists walk through Colombia's dense coastal rain forest. They are looking for a golden poison frog, the most poisonous frog and one of the most toxic animals on the planet.[19] A conservationist spots the small, bright-yellow frog in the soil. He catches it with his bare hands. Now that the frog is caught, it will soon begin to release poison through its skin to protect itself.

The conservationist hands the frog to a researcher wearing gloves, which will protect her from the secretions. If the poison enters the bloodstream, it will lead to heart failure and death. A single frog produces enough poison to kill approximately ten humans.[20] Researching these frogs is important for human medicine. Scientists believe that understanding the toxins these frogs produce could help with the creation of muscle relaxants, anesthetics, and more.

APPEARANCE AND POISON

Juvenile golden poison frogs are black with gold stripes on their backs. As they mature, the shade of black changes until their bodies are a single bright color. Adults are typically bright yellow, but they also come in bright green or orange, and a few are even white. The bright color warns predators that the frog is poisonous. Adults' feet are typically black on the bottom. The toes are not webbed. The eyes and nostrils are also black.

Scientists don't know exactly how the frog's poison originates. But they suspect that some of the insects the frogs eat in the wild consume plants that have the poison. Because of how poisonous the frogs are, they have few predators. One snake, the fire-bellied snake, is resistant to the poison and eats young golden poison frogs. Native peoples of Colombia, including the Chocó people, have long used the poison of these frogs for hunting. People would catch live frogs and rub the tips of blowgun darts on the frogs' backs. Animals hit with these darts would die.

GOLDEN POISON FROG

BEHAVIORS AND THREATS

Golden poison frogs are active during the day and live on the ground. A female lays her eggs on the ground. When the eggs hatch, the male carries the tadpoles on his back to shallow water. Then the tadpoles are on their own.

The frog flicks out its long, sticky tongue to capture prey. Sometimes, when hunting or when courting a mate, the frog will tap its middle toe in excitement. The frogs also communicate

FUN FACT

Captive golden poison frogs are typically much less toxic than wild frogs or aren't toxic at all. This is because they don't eat the insects that are the toxin's source.

with one another. Males call for females using a single long trill. The frogs communicate dominance by pushing up their bodies. They indicate submission by lowering their heads.

Golden poison frogs are an endangered species. Their numbers are dropping largely because of deforestation for agriculture. They also face danger from poaching. Laws make it illegal to take these frogs from the wild. And captive breeders reduce the demand for poached, wild-caught frogs. The local government has also designated the area where the frogs live as protected land. Conservationists are working to further protect this species.

A male golden poison frog carries newly hatched tadpoles on his back.

GOLDEN POISON FROG
Phyllobates terribilis

SIZE
Up to 1.9 inches (4.7 cm) long for females; up to 1.8 inches (4.5 cm) long for males

WEIGHT
Less than 1 ounce (28 g)

RANGE
Colombia's Pacific coast

HABITAT
Lowlands of Amazon rain forest

DIET
Mostly ants; occasionally other invertebrates

LIFE SPAN
Up to 5 years in captivity; likely longer in the wild

GOLIATH FROG

Goliath frogs are the largest frogs in the world, with their bodies reaching up to 12.6 inches (32 cm) long. A watch next to the frog helps show its massive size.

It is nighttime in Cameroon. A male goliath frog the length of an American football digs into the rocks on the bank of a river. The frog pushes rocks away from the center of the hole, creating a nest that is 3.3 feet (1 m) wide and four inches (10 cm) deep.[21] Some of the rocks the frog moves are half his weight. Once the frog has finished his nest pool, which has rims rising out of the water to protect the pool from currents, the nest is ready for eggs. A female lays hundreds of eggs in the pool. Then she stays and guards the nest for a time, clearing leaves and other debris from the pool.

APPEARANCE

The goliath frog is the largest of all living frogs. Its head is triangular, and its body is somewhat flattened. The frog's skin is bumpy and greenish brown. The belly skin is yellowish green. Its back feet are webbed, and its long hind legs are powerful.

There is still much to be learned about goliath frogs. Males are larger than females, which is unusual for frogs. Scientists think this may be because males are the ones who build nests. They need to be large to move rocks. The nest-building behavior may also be why these frogs are so large in general.

When tadpoles hatch from their eggs, they are approximately the same size as the tadpoles of

GOLIATH FROG

an average frog. But they grow much larger over the next two to three months. After metamorphosis, young frogs still spend much of their time in the water. Older adults will occasionally bask in the sunlight on rocks or other objects jutting out from the water.

PREDATOR AND PREY

Goliath frogs eat many types of animals, including insects, crustaceans, fish, small mammals, and amphibians. They hunt at night, both on land and in the water. When in the water, they attack prey at the water's surface.

With its legs extended, the goliath frog can measure up to 2.5 feet (75 cm) long.

FUN FACT

Unlike many other frogs, goliath frogs do not have vocal sacs. However, they can still make a whistling noise by opening their mouths.

Freshwater shrimp prey on the eggs of these frogs, but little is known about the predators of the adult frogs. Humans are the only known predators, though scientists believe other animals likely eat the frogs. The color of the frogs' skin helps camouflage them among mossy rocks. These frogs typically stay near water. To escape from potential threats, the frogs leap into the water. They are slow and easy to catch on land, often tiring after just six leaps.[22]

Because of the goliath frog's size, some people hunt them for food. Others keep the frogs as pets. The frog is classified as endangered. Being hunted for food and habitat destruction are the primary threats to this species. Local captive breeding programs are working to boost the population. In addition, laws limit the number of frogs that can be exported.

GOLIATH FROG
Conraua goliath

SIZE
6.7–12.6 inches (17–32 cm) long from nose to vent

WEIGHT
1.3–7.3 pounds (0.6–3.3 kg)

RANGE
Equatorial Guinea, Cameroon

HABITAT
Humid, hot rain forests with fast-flowing rivers and waterfalls

DIET
Insects, crustaceans, other invertebrates; fish, small mammals, amphibians

LIFE SPAN
Up to 15 years in the wild; up to 5 years in captivity

HELLBENDER

The hellbender may have gotten its common name from people who thought the salamander looked like it was from hell and bent on returning there.

Researchers in Virginia wade into a stream. They wear goggles and snorkels. The team is looking for a hellbender salamander nest. The researchers locate a square artificial nesting box at the bottom of the stream. Working underwater, they lift the top off the box to reveal a male hellbender guarding a mass of eggs. He walks around the bundle of eggs, stirring up the water so they can get oxygen.

The researchers carefully pull the eggs into a bucket. The eggs are attached to one another by a white material, and they come out of the box like rope. Then the researchers capture the male. They take photos of the eggs so they can count them.

They examine the male and draw blood from him to make sure he is healthy. Then they place the father and eggs back in the box. Their research will help them understand whether the hellbenders in this stream are healthy. This information will tell them whether the stream habitat itself is healthy.

SLIPPERY SALAMANDERS

Hellbenders are aquatic salamanders that live in streams for their whole lives. Their bodies are somewhat flattened in shape, and their dark-brown or black skin has many loose folds, including a loose flap of skin running along each side of the salamander. These folds increase the surface area of the skin to help them get more oxygen from the water. The skin is particularly slimy, making them hard to catch as well as making them taste bad to predators.

The hellbender's tail is flattened vertically, and the salamander uses it to help it swim through the water. It keeps some traits of its larval form, including small, lidless eyes and gill slits. Larvae have external gills and grow to

FUN FACT

The hellbender's slimy skin has inspired some people to call it the snot otter.

HELLBENDER

twice their hatching size in the first year.[23] They do not have limbs when they hatch, but the limbs develop as they grow. By two years old, they have lost their external gills.[24] They become mature adults between the ages of three and six years old.[25]

BEHAVIOR AND CONSERVATION

The hellbender is a solitary animal. It typically hunts at night and takes shelter under streambed rocks during the day. Its eyesight is poor, so it relies on its ability to sense movement in the water and its sense of smell to find prey.

Hellbenders are near threatened. Their numbers are declining, and they could soon be at risk of extinction. They need clean water to breathe, and clean water is becoming harder to find. Human development is causing sediment to build up in streams, making water murky. In addition, chemicals and toxins are present in many streams. Some zoos have started captive breeding programs to try to help maintain numbers. There are also some protected habitat areas, a designation that helps keep streams in those areas clean.

HELLBENDER
Cryptobranchus alleganiensis

SIZE
1–2.3 feet (29.5–68.6 cm) long from nose to tail

WEIGHT
0.9–2.2 pounds (0.4–1 kg)

RANGE
Appalachian Mountains from southwestern New York to northern Georgia and Alabama

HABITAT
Freshwater streams with large rocks and other objects for shelter

DIET
Mainly crayfish; occasionally insects, fish, smaller salamanders

LIFE SPAN
12–15 years on average in the wild; up to 29 years in captivity

JEFFERSON SALAMANDER

Jefferson salamanders face predation from snakes, owls, raccoons, and skunks.

The Jefferson salamander walks through fallen leaves on the forest floor. Suddenly it notices a snake flicking its tongue nearby. Feeling threatened, the salamander raises its tail and thrashes it in the air. Glands in the tail release a poisonous substance. The snake is still focused on the salamander, so in a desperate move, the salamander sheds its tail. Muscles in the detached tail cause it to twitch, and this movement distracts the snake while the salamander flees to its burrow.

APPEARANCE AND LIFESTYLE

The Jefferson salamander is dark gray or brown with blue spots on its sides, legs, and tail. The head is short and rounded. Its tail is almost as long as its body. Males have longer tails than females, but females are larger overall.

This species is one of approximately 30 mole salamanders, named because they typically live underground or under fallen leaves.[26] Because adult Jefferson salamanders spend most of their time under cover, scientists know little about their diets. But the salamanders likely eat worms and other animals in the soil.

FUN FACT

The Jefferson salamander was named for Jefferson College in Pennsylvania, which was named for the third US president, Thomas Jefferson.

JEFFERSON SALAMANDER

The salamanders breed in ponds, but they spend most of their time on land. They pass the winter in burrows. They become inactive during this time, using less energy until temperatures warm again.

Jefferson salamander larvae have external gills that disappear as they age.

BREEDING

Jefferson salamanders breed in early spring. As the rain begins to fall, the salamanders travel to breeding pools. Males leave packets of sperm on the ground. Females pick up the packets with their cloacae. Females lay their eggs a day or two later, attaching them to underwater objects such as sticks. They are placed deep enough that, if the surface water freezes, they stay in liquid water.

Larvae will hatch in two to 14 weeks, depending on the water temperature.[27] A larva has a tail fin and external gills, and its skin is yellowish green with dark spots. Larvae darken in color as they age. They hide in vegetation during the day and hunt for food at night. Larvae will eat many kinds of prey, including other salamander larvae. A few months after hatching, they complete metamorphosis. They lose their gills, leave the water, and rely on their lungs to breathe. They will be able to have their own offspring in two or three years.[28]

JEFFERSON SALAMANDER
Ambystoma jeffersonianum

SIZE
4.2–8.3 inches (10.7–21 cm) long from nose to tail

WEIGHT
Unavailable

RANGE
Southern New England to Indiana, Kentucky, West Virginia, Virginia

HABITAT
Areas with ponds, especially moist upland forests

DIET
Larvae eat zooplankton, aquatic insect larvae, snails, other aquatic prey; adults eat insects, slugs, worms, other prey they can swallow

LIFE SPAN
6 years on average in the wild; likely longer in captivity

LESSER SIREN

Lesser sirens can be found in the eastern United States and Mexico.

A long, gray creature swims through a shallow pond in Indiana. Its flexible body ripples in an S shape, then bends into a U as it turns. The creature resembles an eel, with a fish-like dorsal fin along its long tail, but it is not a fish. A set of feathery gills waves on either side of the animal's head. It does not have hind legs, but just behind the gills are two short, small front legs. This animal is a lesser siren, an aquatic freshwater salamander.

HABITAT AND SURVIVAL

The lesser siren makes its home in shallow, warm, fresh water with dense vegetation. These habitats can include marshes, farm ponds, and drainage ditches. Sirens are able to get enough oxygen to survive even from water with relatively low oxygen levels, allowing them to thrive in these habitats.

Sometimes the shallow waters dry up for a period of time. The lesser siren can estivate, or become dormant. It burrows into the mud, often using existing crayfish holes. If the mud begins to dry out, the siren produces a mucus that forms a cocoon around its body

The lesser siren can thrive in habitats that do not have enough oxygen for other species.

LESSER SIREN

and helps keep moisture locked in. Its metabolism slows down, and it relies on body fat to survive the period of dormancy. Lesser sirens can also travel short distances over land to other bodies of water. They use their tiny front legs to pull themselves along.

DIET AND REPRODUCTION

Lesser sirens search for food along the bottoms of their ponds or other water habitats. They stir up the material on the bottom and eat the prey living there, including insects and tadpoles. The sirens are important predators in their habitats, helping control the populations of other species. Scientists do not know much about the

FUN FACT

The lesser siren's tail can make up as much as 40 percent of its total length.[29]

predators of lesser sirens, but they believe some snakes, fish, birds, and alligators eat these amphibians. Lesser sirens will sometimes let out distress cries when caught by predators.

Little is known about the breeding behaviors of lesser sirens. Captive breeding attempts have been mostly unsuccessful. However, scientists have found bite marks on sirens during mating season, leading to the belief that breeding may be aggressive. Hatchlings are born with dark stripes and fully formed front legs.

LESSER SIREN
Siren intermedia

SIZE
0.59–2.3 feet (18–69 cm) long from nose to tail

WEIGHT
1.8 ounces (50 g) on average

RANGE
Eastern United States and Mexico

HABITAT
Calm, shallow waters; swamps with dense vegetation

DIET
Small aquatic organisms, amphibian larvae

LIFE SPAN
6 years on average in captivity

MEXICAN AXOLOTL

The Mexican axolotl is usually dark brown but can be white.

A Mexican axolotl swims in Lake Xochimilco near Mexico City, Mexico. Its finned tail propels it through the water. Suddenly a large fish lunges at the salamander and bites its leg off. But the axolotl won't be without that leg forever. Very quickly, blood clots at the site of the wound, keeping the animal from bleeding out. Cells form a protective layer around the wound. That layer of cells grows over a few days, and underneath that layer, a cone-shaped collection of cells called a blastema forms. These blastema cells multiply and begin rebuilding the bone, muscle, skin, and other tissues of the leg. Within a few months, the axolotl has a fully formed new leg.

The axolotl has the ability to regenerate not only limbs but also its spinal cord, heart, and other organs. This excites researchers. They hope to learn more about the axolotl's regenerative abilities in order to improve the lives of people who have lost limbs.

APPEARANCE AND BREEDING

The Mexican axolotl is an aquatic salamander that usually retains larval traits throughout its life and does not go through metamorphosis. It has feathery external gills and tail fins, and it lacks eyelids. This salamander has lungs, but it relies mainly on its gills to breathe. Axolotls are typically a dark brownish-green with mottling, though they may also be albino. The shape of an axolotl's mouth can give it the appearance of grinning.

When mating, a male axolotl shakes his tail and releases a sperm mass. The female positions herself over that sperm mass, shakes her tail, and takes in the sperm mass through her cloaca. She then lays a few hundred eggs, which are attached to underwater objects such as rocks. A few weeks later, the young hatch and are independent.

Axolotls are popular pets.

FOOD AND THREATS

Mexican axolotls are native to just two high-altitude lakes near Mexico City. One has been drained. Axolotls still live in the other, Lake Xochimilco, which is threatened with pollution. The amphibians were originally the top predators of their habitats, eating many animals from fish to mollusks and arthropods. But large fish have been introduced to the lake and sometimes prey on the salamanders. Due to the loss of habitat and the threat from introduced predators, the axolotl population is shrinking. The salamander is now critically endangered.

Many people are working to protect the species. Some work on ways to purify the water in Lake Xochimilco. In addition, axolotls are already bred in captivity for both laboratory research and as pets. More habitat restoration is needed to help save this species in the wild.

FUN FACT

Axolotl means "water dog" in the Aztec Nahuatl language. The species is connected to the god Xolotl, who is said to have turned himself into one.

MEXICAN AXOLOTL
Ambystoma mexicanum

SIZE
9 inches (23 cm) long on average

WEIGHT
2.1–3.9 ounces (60–110 g)

RANGE
Lake Xochimilco near Mexico City, Mexico

HABITAT
Channels and deeper areas of Lake Xochimilco

DIET
Any food it can catch, such as arthropods, fish, mollusks

LIFE SPAN
10–12 years in the wild; up to 15 years in captivity

MIMIC POISON FROG

A mimic poison frog's color patterns match those of a more toxic poison frog species. This helps protect it from predators.

It has been two weeks since the three mimic poison frog tadpoles hatched from their eggs. They swim in small pools of water that formed on nearby plants. But now it is time for them to move. The father frog puts one tadpole on his back. The tadpole is very small, gray, and has two dark eyes. The father hops off, carrying the tadpole to a new pool of water in a plant. He returns for a second tadpole, carrying this one to a different pool of water. Then he brings the last one to a third pool of water.

MIMIC POISON FROG

The pools these tadpoles live in have little food. The parents must feed them. The mother frog approaches a pool. The hungry tadpole wiggles its tail frantically. Then the female lays an unfertilized egg for the tadpole to eat. She will continue feeding the tadpoles for months until the young can leave the pools.

IMITATING OTHERS

The mimic poison frog is a species of poison dart frog. Like other poison frogs, it produces a poison to deter predators, though the poison is milder than that of other frogs.

Its bright skin colors serve as a warning to other predators that it is poisonous. The mimic poison frog's color patterns are what earned the species its name. This frog can come in one of three different color patterns. Each pattern closely resembles the color pattern of a different, deadlier poison dart frog species in its range. It is the only known amphibian species that mimics more than one other species.[30]

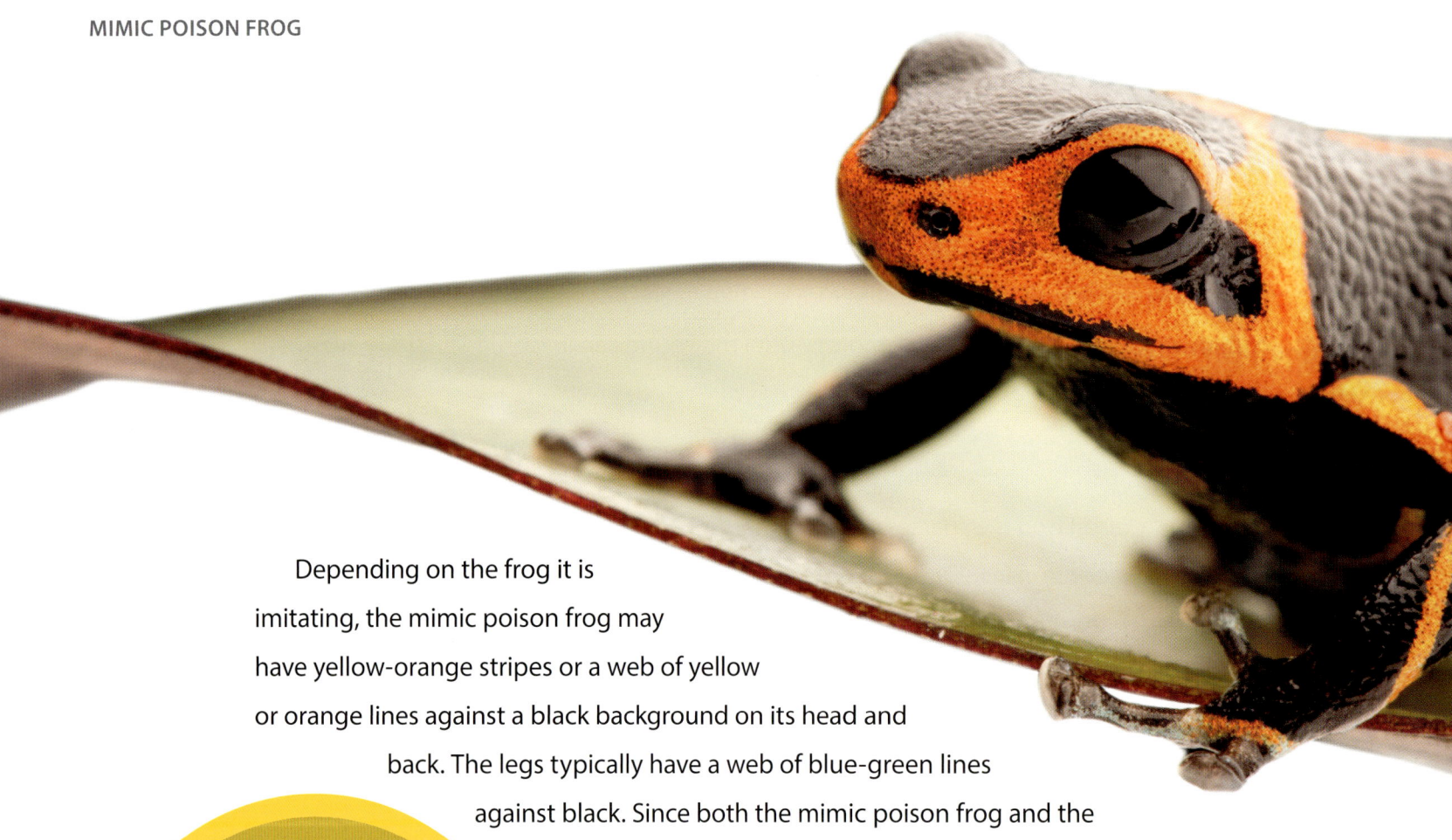

MIMIC POISON FROG

Depending on the frog it is imitating, the mimic poison frog may have yellow-orange stripes or a web of yellow or orange lines against a black background on its head and back. The legs typically have a web of blue-green lines against black. Since both the mimic poison frog and the species it imitates are poisonous, the imitation is beneficial for all of the frog species. A predator that has encountered one species may avoid its look-alike.

FUN FACT
A mimic poison frog typically prefers to mate with another frog that mimics the same species it does.

BEHAVIOR

Mimic poison frogs are the only amphibians known to be monogamous. This means that a frog breeds with only one other frog during a mating season. Scientists think these frogs are monogamous because both parents are needed to raise the young.

The frogs are active during the day. They spend their time in the trees, taking shelter in the shade during the hottest part of the day. The species faces a few challenges, including loss of habitat to human development. However, its population is believed to be stable, and conservation groups do not list it as a species threatened with extinction.

MIMIC POISON FROG
Ranitomeya imitator

SIZE
0.67–0.87 inches (1.7–2.2 cm) long from nose to vent

WEIGHT
0.044 ounces (1.25 g) on average

RANGE
Peru

HABITAT
Eastern foothills of the Andes in wet mountain forests, tropical lowland moist forests

DIET
Ants, beetles, flies, other invertebrates

LIFE SPAN
3–10 years

OLM

An olm cannot see; its eyes only detect light and dark.

Deep in a dark Slovenian cave, a pale creature lurks in a shallow pool of water. It slowly crawls over the stones at the bottom of the pool. Small fingers on each foot grip the rocks, and its short, thin legs push it along. This aquatic salamander is an olm. It is hunting for its next meal. Sight won't help the olm. The cave is too dark, and its eyes—covered in a layer of skin—can only sense light and dark. Instead, sensors in its ears detect small vibrations in the water. It follows the vibrations to a cluster of insect larvae, and it begins eating. When the olm is finished eating, it rests at the bottom of the pool. Food is scarce in this cave. It may be up to ten years before its next meal.[31]

LIVING IN THE DARK

The olm has a long, thin body. The head is wide, narrowing a bit at the snout but coming to a blunt end. A few olms have dark skin, but most have white skin, sometimes with a pink tint. But these white olms are not albino. If exposed to sunlight, the skin will become dark.

Behind the skull sit pink, feathery external gills, and just behind those are two front legs. The salamander's torso is very

FUN FACT
Europeans once thought olms were baby dragons because of their long, snake-like bodies.

long, with two hind legs extending near the end of the torso. The tail has fins along the top and bottom to help the creature move in the water.

Because the calm cave pools do not have much oxygen, the olm breathes with both its gills and its lungs. In addition to being able to sense movement in the water, the olm has an excellent sense of smell, which it also uses to find prey. The olm has taste buds in its mouth and near the gills. The taste buds by the olm's gills may help it taste prey in the water.

CAVE LIFE

There is still much to learn about olms because their remote habitats make them challenging to study. But scientists know some things about the olm's life from researching captive specimens. After mating, the female goes off on her own and lays up to 70 eggs beneath rocks in the water.[32] She guards the eggs. Larvae hatch in a few months. The exact time is based on the water temperature, which also determines how quickly larvae develop. It may take up to 14 years for them to become sexually mature. Olms do not undergo a noticeable metamorphosis. They live very long lives, sometimes surviving for more than 100 years.[33]

Olms do not have any natural predators. They are at the top of the food chain in the cave systems in which they live. But they face threats from humans. Pollution threatens the water in which they live. They are also taken illegally to be kept as pets. The olm's numbers are dropping, and the species is considered vulnerable, meaning it could become endangered soon. National parks and other protected lands provide safe habitats for these animals.

OLM
Proteus anguinus

SIZE
0.7–1 feet (20–30 cm) long from nose to tail

WEIGHT
0.7 ounces (20 g) on average

RANGE
Countries along the Adriatic Sea, including Slovenia, Italy, Bosnia and Herzegovina, Croatia

HABITAT
Freshwater lakes and streams within limestone mountain caves

DIET
Mostly insects, but occasionally any other invertebrate that fits in its mouth

LIFE SPAN
68.5 years on average in the wild and captivity, up to 100 years or more

ORIENTAL FIRE-BELLIED TOAD

Oriental fire-bellied toads face a lot of competition at breeding sites.

A male oriental fire-bellied toad floats in the water of the stream and calls for a female. But there is a lot of competition. He is joined by several other males at the breeding site, all looking for a mate. There are more males than females here. The male notices a toad swimming by. He jumps onto the toad's back. It is another male, who lets out a croak of protest. The toad lets go and keeps searching. He spots another toad and jumps onto its back. This time, it is a female.

The female keeps swimming, and the male grips her just above her hind legs. She lays eggs on underwater plants near the shore. As she lays the eggs, the male fertilizes them. Then the parents part ways. The eggs are left to develop and hatch on their own.

APPEARANCE

The oriental fire-bellied toad's back is brownish gray to bright green with dark spots. Its belly, which inspires its common name, ranges from bright reddish orange to yellow with dark spots. The pupils are triangular in shape.

The two sexes look similar, but males are usually smaller than females.

FUN FACT

During breeding season, males may be so excitable that they mistake twigs, plants, and other animals for female toads.

ORIENTAL FIRE-BELLIED TOAD

78

Males develop spiny pads on their first and second fingers to help them grip females during breeding season. Males typically have rougher skin and develop thicker forearms when they are ready to breed.

BEHAVIOR AND DEFENSE

Adult oriental fire-bellied toads live on land and eat many kinds of invertebrates. These toads rely primarily on their sight to hunt. A toad sits and watches for movement, waiting for prey to come close. The colors of its back provide camouflage against the wet, muddy environment. Once the prey is close, the toad pounces, grabbing the prey in its mouth.

Birds and larger aquatic animals eat these toads. The same coloring that camouflages the toad while it hunts also helps keep it hidden from predators. But the toad has another defense. Its skin produces toxins. If the toad is seen by a predator, it stands up tall, arching its back. This reveals the brightly colored belly. The toad may even flip onto its back, exposing the belly in full. The color warns the predator that the toad is poisonous. Predators are less likely to eat the toad.

ORIENTAL FIRE-BELLIED TOAD
Bombina orientalis

SIZE
1.4–3.1 inches (3.5–8 cm) from nose to vent

WEIGHT
1–2 ounces (28–57 g)

RANGE
Northeastern China, North Korea, South Korea, Thailand, southern Japan

HABITAT
High-elevation forests, river valleys, swampy bushlands, open meadows; near lakes, ponds, swamps, streams, springs, puddles, ditches

DIET
Larvae eat algae, fungi, plants, other organic matter; adults eat land invertebrates such as worms, insects

LIFE SPAN
Up to 20 years in the wild; up to 30 years in captivity

RED-EYED TREE FROG

Red-eyed tree frogs are excellent climbers.

A bright-green frog with big, red eyes hangs on the underside of a large, wet leaf in a rain forest in Costa Rica. She is a red-eyed tree frog. Her large, rounded toes keep her suctioned to the leaf. They support not only her weight but also the weight of her smaller mate, who is hanging from her back. The female lays her eggs on the leaf one at a time. The male fertilizes each one as it is laid.

After laying a group of eggs, the female frog needs to return to the water and fill her bladder to keep her eggs hydrated. With the male still on her back, she departs the leaf and finds water. Once she is hydrated, she and the male lay another group of eggs on a leaf overhanging the water. The eggs are opaque and clustered in a clear, jelly-like substance. But after a few days, the eggs become clear, and the tadpoles are visible. They wiggle around in their eggs. In a few more days, they hatch from their eggs, dropping into the water below.

STARTLING APPEARANCE

The red-eyed tree frog has a green topside. It typically has blue sides and orange feet. Its skin is smooth, and the body is slender for a frog. Toe pads that act similar to suction cups help it cling to various surfaces in its environment, making it an excellent climber, an important ability for the tree-dwelling species.

Although this frog is colorful, it is not poisonous. It has another defense. The tree frog sleeps during the day. The lower lid of each

The red-eyed tree frog's translucent eyelids allow it to startle predators with its eyes.

eye is transparent, with a webbing of gold lines that hides the bright red color of the eyes. But if a predator startles the frog awake, the frog's eyes pop open. Scientists think the sudden opening of the large red eyes startles predators. Then the frog can hop away.

GROWING UP

Tree frog eggs face predation from snakes and insects. More than half of a red-eyed tree frog's eggs fall prey to snakes and wasps.[34] Tadpoles will hatch early when disturbed by predators,

> **FUN FACT**
> Some young red-eyed tree frogs can change color. They are green during the day. At night, they become somewhat purple or reddish brown.

allowing some to get away. After tadpoles hatch and drop into the water, they are at risk of being eaten by fish and other aquatic animals.

Once the tadpoles develop their adult bodies, they do not have red eyes right away. Their eyes are yellow for the first two weeks. Then the eyes begin turning red over a few days.

These frogs are not currently at risk of becoming extinct. But their numbers are declining. Deforestation, pollution, and climate change are all threats to these frogs.

RED-EYED TREE FROG
Agalychnis callidryas

SIZE
Up to 2 inches (5 cm) long from nose to vent for males; up to 3 inches (8 cm) long for females

WEIGHT
0.2–0.5 ounces (6–15 g)

RANGE
Throughout Central America, into Mexico

HABITAT
Tropical rain forests, typically lowland rain forests

DIET
Insects, including crickets, moths, flies, grasshoppers; occasionally smaller frogs

LIFE SPAN
5 years on average in the wild; 4.1 years on average in captivity

RINGED CAECILIAN

Scientists still have much to learn about ringed caecilians.

The ringed caecilian burrows into the moist soil in Ecuador. It is searching for a meal. The legless, worm-like amphibian contracts and relaxes muscles in its body to push itself forward. It finds a cricket in the soil. The caecilian bites down on the cricket with its sharp teeth. As it bites, it releases a substance that seems to immobilize the cricket. This is important since the caecilian does not have legs to hold the insect and keep it from escaping. Now the caecilian can gulp down its prey whole.

A SNAKE-LIKE AMPHIBIAN

Ringed caecilians, like most other caecilians, are not well understood. Because they spend much of their time underground, these creatures are challenging to study. The results of research on ringed caecilians published in 2020 noted that the glands in their mouths are similar to a snake's venom glands.[35] The substance they secrete contains a protein that is common in some snake venom. More research is needed to confirm the exact use of the substance. If verified, the ringed caecilian would be the first known venomous amphibian.

The ringed caecilian is long and limbless. Its head is narrow. There are

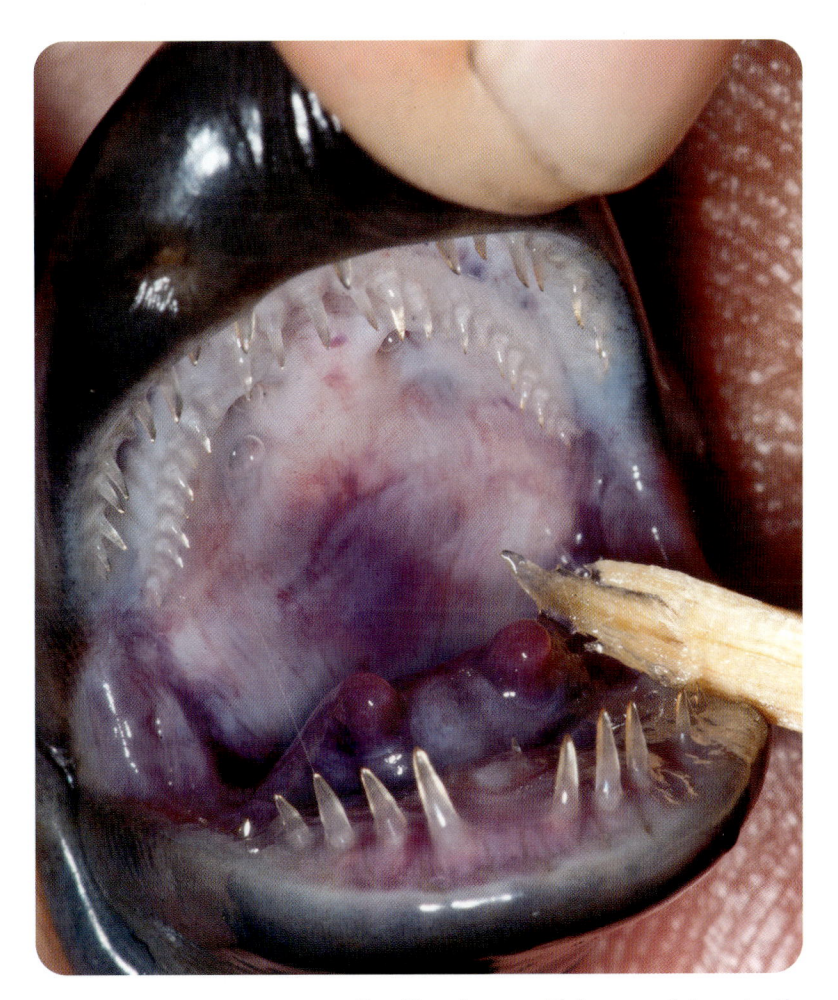

Caecilians have multiple rows of sharp teeth.

RINGED CAECILIAN

two rows of sharp teeth on the top jaw and one row on the bottom. It has small eyes, and a short tentacle near each eye helps it feel its surroundings. Its skin is bluish black or gray. Cream or white grooves ring the body. The caecilian does not have a tail. The vent, where its body releases digestive waste, is at the very end of the body.

GROWING UP

A female caecilian lays eggs in a nest among the roots of a tree. The mother curls around the eggs. When the young hatch, they feed on the outer layer of the mother's skin, which has become rich in nutrients. The young feed in a frenzy, competing with each other over pieces of the skin. The mother calmly lies still. She does not eat during the time she is caring for her young.

Ringed caecilians will burrow up to 7.9 inches (20 cm) deep in the soil.[36] They eat food found in the soil, including insects and other invertebrates. The caecilians have several predators, including ants, mammals, and snakes. The caecilian's skin produces toxic secretions that can cause paralysis or death. This helps protect the amphibians from predators. There is little known about the population of ringed caecilians, but their broad range means they are not considered to be at risk of extinction.

FUN FACT
Young caecilians eat fluid that comes from the mother's vent. Scientists do not yet know why they do this.

RINGED CAECILIAN
Siphonops annulatus

SIZE
1–1.5 feet (29–45 cm) long

WEIGHT
Unavailable

RANGE
Argentina, Bolivia, Brazil, Colombia, Ecuador, French Guiana, Guyana, Paraguay, Peru, Suriname, Venezuela

HABITAT
Mainly damp habitats with a lot of organic matter and invertebrates

DIET
Invertebrates that live in the soil including crickets, snails, slugs, termites, worms

LIFE SPAN
Unavailable

ROUGH-SKINNED NEWT

The rough-skinned newt's bumpy skin is the basis of its common name.

The rough-skinned newt climbs along mossy rocks near a forest pond. It is hunting for food. It spots a slug on the rock. The newt creeps over, then snatches up the slug in its jaws. It gulps down its meal and keeps walking. Suddenly it notices a garter snake nearby. The newt stretches its neck and tail up to reveal its bright-orange belly. This color is a warning to the predator that the newt is very toxic. But the garter snake is resistant to the newt's poison. The snake strikes, capturing the newt and swallowing it headfirst.

APPEARANCE AND HABITAT

The rough-skinned newt has a thick body with brownish skin on its back. Most of the time its skin is dry and bumpy, giving the rough-skinned newt its name. But during breeding season, the male's skin becomes smooth and slimy.

Larvae are aquatic. A larva's tail fin runs from its shoulders down to the tip of its tail. Adults divide their time between the land and water. They typically spend the most time on land, hiding under rotting wood. But they return to the water during spring breeding season, and they may live in the water during the dry summer months. A few adults spend their whole lives in water, and some even keep their external gills.

PREDATORS AND DEFENSES

The rough-skinned newt has few natural predators. It is extremely toxic, with enough toxin in some individuals to kill tens of thousands of mice.[37] The level of toxin varies by region, however. Some populations are not very toxic. Others are more toxic than the extremely deadly golden poison frog.

One of the newt's only predators, the common garter snake, is resistant to this toxin. Scientists believe the presence of the garter snake influences the varying toxin levels in the newt. Newts that live in areas without garter snakes are not very toxic. But newt populations that are preyed upon by garter snakes have high toxin levels. Likewise, garter snakes that live in areas where rough-skinned newts are absent do not have a resistance to the toxin. This indicates that the two species influence one another. As garter snakes develop resistance to the toxin levels, the newts must become even more toxic to deter the snakes. The snakes then develop resistance to the stronger levels of toxins.

FUN FACT

The rough-skinned newt produces a toxin called tetrodotoxin. Puffer fish and blue-ringed octopuses also produce this toxin.

ROUGH-SKINNED NEWT
Taricha granulosa

SIZE
5–8.5 inches (12.7–21.6 cm) long from nose to tail

WEIGHT
0.43 ounces (12.2 g)

RANGE
North American Pacific Coast, from southeastern Alaska to central California

HABITAT
Bodies of calm water, including ponds and lakes, located in forested hills and mountains

DIET
Many animals including snails, insects, other amphibians

LIFE SPAN
12 years on average in the wild

TOMATO FROG

Tomato frogs can puff themselves up with air when threatened.

An orangish-yellow tomato frog hops through a garden in Madagascar. Suddenly a snake comes slithering into view. The tomato frog stops moving and begins breathing in air. That air fills its lungs, but the frog also forces the air into other parts of its body. The frog puffs larger and larger with each breath of air. Its body is now much too large for the snake to swallow. The slithering predator will have to find a meal elsewhere.

APPEARANCE AND HABITAT

The tomato frog is named for its appearance. Its skin color can make it look similar to tomatoes. Females are more of an orangish red, while males are more yellowish orange. Their toes are not webbed. A black stripe runs from the back corner of each eye to the abdomen.

This species lives only in the northeastern part of the African island of Madagascar. It can live in a variety of habitats, as long as there is loose soil into which it can burrow. The frogs can even live in certain urban areas.

Frogs breed year-round after rainfall. The female lays thousands of eggs in shallow, calm water.[38] Tadpoles are black to tan in color. They undergo metamorphosis in approximately one month, and they start turning red a few months later. They are able to reproduce at two or three years old.[39]

TOMATO FROG

DON'T EAT THIS TOMATO

The ability to puff up isn't the only defense the tomato frog has. It can also burrow quickly into the soil. It hides there with only its eyes exposed. The frog may burrow while waiting for prey to come close enough to catch, or it may burrow to hide from predators.

In addition, the frog's skin produces a sticky secretion when the frog is threatened. The secretion forms a white lather on

FUN FACT
The sticky substance on the tomato frog's back has more holding force than the same amount of contact cement.

the frog's back. The substance can cause numbing and irritation to any predator that tries to eat the frog, and it can even lead to severe allergic reactions or respiratory failure.

There is still a lot to learn about the tomato frog. It is currently considered not to be at risk of becoming endangered. But its numbers are decreasing. Its main threat is habitat destruction due to human development and pollution. Captive breeding programs mean there is little demand for wild-caught frogs for the pet trade, so there is little threat to the frogs from poaching.

TOMATO FROG
Dyscophus antongilii

SIZE
2.4–4.1 inches (6–10.5 cm) from nose to vent

WEIGHT
0.9 ounces (26 g) on average

RANGE
Northeastern Madagascar

HABITAT
Rain forests, wooded coastal areas, wet or dry underbrush, urban areas

DIET
Small invertebrates

LIFE SPAN
3–11 years in the wild; 3–12 years or more in captivity

WALLACE'S FLYING FROG

Webbing between the Wallace's flying frog's toes allows it to glide from tree to tree.

A Wallace's flying frog climbs through the treetops in Malaysia. It comes to the end of a branch. The next tree is 50 feet (15 m) away. But this is not a problem for the little frog. It leaps into the air toward the tree, stretching its long fingers and toes wide to reveal full webbing. The frog holds its feet parallel to the ground so the webbing can catch air and act like a parachute, allowing the frog to glide all the way to the distant tree.

When the frog reaches a branch, its toes press onto the wood. The pads are large and help cushion the landing. Special bones help press the suction cup–like toe pads into the branch so the frog doesn't fall off. The frog then crawls along the branch to continue on its way.

APPEARANCE AND GLIDING

Wallace's flying frog has large eyes and a wide head. Its skin is a smooth, shiny green on the back. The sides, toe pads, and snout are yellow. The webbing between the frog's toe pads is black. In addition to webbing between the toes, there are also two flaps of skin on each arm. One is along the inner edge of the arm, and the other is on the outer edge of the forearm and the foot. On the hind legs, another flap runs from the heel to the vent.

Despite its name, the frog cannot fly. It cannot maintain elevation in the air. Rather, it glides, using its webbed feet to slow its descent so it can travel longer distances in the air than it could if it simply jumped. When scientists discovered this frog in the mid-1800s, it was the first time the scientific community had heard of a gliding frog. Today there are a few other known species of gliding frogs.

BEHAVIOR

Wallace's flying frog spends most of its time in the trees. But when it is ready to breed, it uses its webbing to glide down closer to the ground. Females lay their eggs in forest pools or animal wallows, including rhinoceros wallows. A wallow is a muddy depression created when animals roll in the dirt.

FUN FACT

This frog species is named after the naturalist Alfred Russel Wallace (1823–1913). Wallace first saw the frog in 1855.[40]

The female finds branches or leaves above one of those small pools of water. Her body produces a fluid, which she beats with her hind legs until it foams, sticking to the branches or leaves. She lays her eggs in the foam, and then the male fertilizes them. When the larvae hatch, they drop into the water, where they live until they complete metamorphosis.

WALLACE'S FLYING FROG
Rhacophorus nigropalmatus

SIZE
3.5–3.9 inches (9–10 cm) from nose to vent

WEIGHT
Unavailable

RANGE
Borneo, Malaysia

HABITAT
Moist tropical forests

DIET
Insects and other small invertebrates

LIFE SPAN
Unavailable

ESSENTIAL FACTS

AMPHIBIAN FEATURES

- All amphibians lack the ability to internally control body temperature. They use their surroundings, such as sunlight and shade, to regulate body temperature.

- An amphibian's skin typically absorbs substances easily and aids with breathing. Many amphibians also produce toxic secretions through their skins.

- Many amphibians go through metamorphosis, a process in which their bodies change in form as they grow and develop.

NOTABLE SPECIES

- The cane toad (*Rhinella marina*) is very toxic and has become highly invasive in Australia, where few native predators have resistance to the toxin.

- The Fleischmann's glass frog (*Hyalinobatrachium fleischmanni*) has translucent skin through which parts of its organs are visible.

- The golden poison frog (*Phyllobates terribilis*) is one of the most toxic animals on Earth.

- The olm (*Proteus anguinus*) is a nearly blind, cave-dwelling salamander that people once thought was a baby dragon.

- The ringed caecilian (*Siphonops annulatus*) is a limbless amphibian that lives mostly in the soil.

AMPHIBIANS' ROLES ON EARTH

Amphibians live on every continent except Antarctica. They are an important part of the food chain in their habitats. The American toad (*Anaxyrus americanus*) helps control insect pests in the United States. Some amphibians, including the Chinese giant salamander (*Andrias davidianus*), are top predators in their habitats. The common mudpuppy (*Necturus maculosus*) is an important source of food for many species. In addition, because amphibians' skins easily absorb substances, the animals are very sensitive to changes in their habitats and can be an early indicator that something is wrong in an ecosystem. Scientists can monitor amphibian populations, and if they are declining, scientists can step in and help. The hellbender (*Cryptobranchus alleganiensis*) is one species being monitored to keep tabs on habitat health.

AMPHIBIANS AND CONSERVATION

Some amphibians, such as the cane toad (*Rhinella marina*), are highly invasive and harm populations of native species. Others, such as the Chinese giant salamander (*Andrias davidianus*), are critically endangered. The fire salamander (*Salamandra salamandra*) is one of many amphibians threated by a form of chytrid fungus. And others, such as the Mexican axolotl (*Ambystoma mexicanum*), are threatened by habitat loss and pollution. Many people are working to protect amphibians by passing laws, starting captive breeding programs, and restoring habitats.

AMPHIBIANS AROUND THE WORLD

ARCTIC OCEAN

NORTH AMERICA

ATLANTIC OCEAN

PACIFIC OCEAN

SOUTH AMERICA

SOUTHERN OCEAN

ANTARCTICA

- **AMERICAN TOAD** — North America
- **EASTERN NEWT** — Eastern Canada and United States
- **AMERICAN BULLFROG** — Native to North America
- **ROUGH-SKINNED NEWT** — North American Pacific Coast
- **COMMON MUDPUPPY** — Southeastern United States to southeastern Canada
- **HELLBENDER** — Appalachian Mountains
- **JEFFERSON SALAMANDER** — Southern New England to Indiana, Kentucky, West Virginia, Virginia
- **MEXICAN AXOLOTL** — Lake Xochimilco, Mexico
- **LESSER SIREN** — Eastern United States and Mexico
- **FLEISCHMANN'S GLASS FROG** — Mexico, Central and South America
- **GOLDEN POISON FROG** — Colombian Pacific coast
- **RED-EYED TREE FROG** — Central America into Mexico
- **MIMIC POISON FROG** — Peru
- **RINGED CAECILIAN** — South America

102

ARCTIC OCEAN

ASIA

EUROPE

OLM
Slovenia, Italy, Bosnia and Herzegovina, Croatia

FIRE SALAMANDER
Central and southern Europe, North Africa, Middle East

CHINESE GIANT SALAMANDER
China

ORIENTAL FIRE-BELLIED TOAD
Eastern Asia

PACIFIC OCEAN

AFRICA

GOLIATH FROG
Equatorial Guinea, Cameroon

WALLACE'S FLYING FROG
Borneo, Malaysia

TOMATO FROG
Northeastern Madagascar

INDIAN OCEAN

CANE TOAD
Invasive in Australia; native to southwestern United States, Central and South America

AUSTRALIA

ATLANTIC OCEAN

103

GLOSSARY

anesthetic
A substance that causes a loss of consciousness or an insensitivity to pain; used to reduce suffering during surgical procedures.

arthropod
An invertebrate animal of the large phylum Arthropoda, which includes insects, spiders, and crustaceans.

cloaca
In many animals, the entry to the reproductive tract as well as where the body expels waste.

dorsal
Having to do with the back of a living thing.

extinction
The state of having completely died out.

gland
A tissue or organ that secretes a substance.

invertebrate
An animal without a spinal column.

ischium
The lower back portion of an animal's pelvic bone.

larva
An immature form of an animal that changes its body form through metamorphosis.

metamorphosis
A change or transformation, such as when tadpoles change into frogs.

mollusk
An invertebrate animal of the phylum Mollusca, which includes snails, clams, and squids.

mottled
Marked with areas of differing colors.

notochord
A flexible rod extending the length of the body of certain organisms.

ulcer
A portion of skin where tissue has been lost or damaged.

vent
The anus of an amphibian and other animals.

vertebrate
An animal with a spinal column and a brain that is part of its nervous system.

ADDITIONAL RESOURCES

SELECTED BIBLIOGRAPHY

"Amphibian Species of the World." *American Museum of Natural History*, 2021. amphibiansoftheworld.amnh.org. Accessed 26 Jan. 2021.

"AmphibiaWeb." *University of California, Berkeley*, 2021, amphibiaweb.org. Accessed 12 Jan. 2021.

"Animal Diversity Web." *University of Michigan Museum of Zoology*, 2020, animaldiversity.org. Accessed 12 Jan. 2021.

FURTHER READINGS

Kallen, Stuart A. *What Is the Impact of Declining Biodiversity?* ReferencePoint, 2021.

Pelleschi, Andrea. *The Evolution of Amphibians*. Abdo, 2019.

Perdew, Laura. *Bringing Back Our Wetlands*. Abdo, 2018.

ONLINE RESOURCES

To learn more about amphibians, please visit **abdobooklinks.com** or scan this QR code. These links are routinely monitored and updated to provide the most current information available.

MORE INFORMATION

For more information on this subject, contact or visit the following organizations:

Amphibian Foundation

4055 Roswell Rd. NE
Atlanta, GA 30342
info@amphibianfoundation.org
562-774-2248
amphibianfoundation.org

The Amphibian Foundation works to help amphibians in the southeastern United States and worldwide.

Association of Zoos & Aquariums

8403 Colesville Rd., Ste. 710
Silver Spring, MD 20910
301-562-0777
aza.org

The Association of Zoos & Aquariums (AZA) is a nonprofit organization that provides accreditation to zoos and aquariums that meet certain standards of care for their animals. In addition, the AZA supports zoos and aquariums helping with amphibian conservation. It also operates FrogWatch USA, a nationwide citizen science program.

SOURCE NOTES

1. Brent Nguyen and John Cavagnaro. "Amphibian Facts." *AmphibiaWeb*, 2021, amphibiaweb.org. Accessed 26 Feb. 2021.

2. "Rana Catesbeiana." *AmphibiaWeb*, 2021, amphibiaweb.org. Accessed 26 Feb. 2021.

3. "American Bullfrog—Lithobates Catesbeianus." *Montana Field Guide*, n.d., fiedguide.mt.gov. Accessed 26 Feb. 2021.

4. Stacey Grossman. "Anaxyrus Americanus." *Animal Diversity Web*, 2002, animaldiversity.org. Accessed 26 Feb. 2021.

5. Lindsay Partymiller. "American Toad (Bufo [Anaxyrus] Americanus)." *Savannah River Ecology Laboratory*, n.d., srelherp.uga.edu. Accessed 26 Feb. 2021.

6. Grossman, "Anaxyrus Americanus."

7. Haley Bowcock et al. "Beastly Bondage: The Costs of Amplexus in Cane Toads (Bufo Marinus)." *Copeia*, vol. 2009, no. 1, 2009, pp. 29–36. *JSTOR*, jstor.org. Accessed 26 Feb. 2021.

8. Bowcock et al., "Beastly Bondage."

9. Lauren Hatch. "Andrias Davidianus." *Animal Diversity Web*, 2020, animaldiversity.org. Accessed 26 Feb. 2021.

10. Hatch, "Andrias Davidianus."

11. Jeffrey B. LeClere. "Necturus Maculosus." *Minnesota Department of Natural Resources: Rare Species Guide*, 2018, dnr.state.mn.us. Accessed 26 Feb. 2021.

12. Erin Siebert. "Necturus Maculosus." *Animal Diversity Web*, 2008, animaldiversity.org. Accessed 26 Feb. 2021.

13. Ann T. Chang and Michelle Koo. "Salamandra Salamandra." *AmphibiaWeb*, 2020, amphibiaweb.org. Accessed 26 Feb. 2021.

14. Ebony Jones. "Hyalinobatrachium Fleischmanni." *Animal Diversity Web,* 2000, animaldiversity.org. Accessed 26 Feb. 2021.

15. Kellie Whittaker. "Hyalinobatrachium Fleischmanni." *AmphibiaWeb*, 2011, amphibiaweb.org. Accessed 26 Feb. 2021.

16. "Centrolenidae." *AmphibiaWeb*, n.d., amphibiaweb.org. Accessed 26 Feb. 2021.

17. Jones, "Hyalinobatrachium Fleischmanni."

18. Jones, "Hyalinobatrachium Fleischmanni."

19. Mariela C. Alvarez and Mary Wiley. "Phyllobates Terribilis." *Animal Diversity Web*, 2011, animaldiversity.org. Accessed 26 Feb. 2021.

20. Kellie Whittaker. "Phyllobates Terribilis." *AmphibiaWeb*, 2013, amphibiaweb.org. Accessed 26 Feb. 2021.

21. Mongabay.com. "World's Largest Frog Moves Heavy Rocks to Build Nests, Study Finds." *Mongabay*, 13 Aug. 2019, news.mongabay.com. Accessed 26 Feb. 2021.

22. Ann T. Chang. "Conraua Goliath." *AmphibiaWeb*, 2020, amphibiaweb.org. Accessed 26 Feb. 2021.

23. "Cryptobranchus Alleganiensis." *AmphibiaWeb*, 2021, amphibiaweb.org. Accessed 26 Feb. 2021.

24. Zeb Pike. "Cryptobranchus Alleganiensis." *Animal Diversity Web*, 2015, animaldiversity.org. Accessed 26 Feb. 2021.

25. Pike, "Cryptobranchus Alleganiensis."

26. Heather Heying. "Ambystomatidae." *Animal Diversity Web*, 2003, animaldiversity.org. Accessed 26 Feb. 2021.

27. Sarah Kipp. "Ambystoma Jeffersonianum." *Animal Diversity Web*, 2000, animaldiversity.org. Accessed 26 Feb. 2021.

28. "Ambystoma Jeffersonianum." *AmphibiaWeb*, 2021, amphibiaweb.org. Accessed 26 Feb. 2021.

29. Meredith J. Mahoney. "Siren Intermedia." *AmphibiaWeb*, 2003, amphibiaweb.org. Accessed 26 Feb. 2021.

30. Ann T. Chang. "Ranitomeya Imitator." *AmphibiaWeb*, 2020, amphibiaweb.org. Accessed 26 Feb. 2021.

31. Bonnie Burton. "One Blind Cave Salamander Stayed Still for a Whopping Seven Years." *CNET*, 5 Feb. 2020, cnet.com. Accessed 26 Feb. 2021.

32. Kellie Whittaker and Michelle S. Koo. "Proteus Anguinus." *AmphibiaWeb*, 2021, amphibiaweb.org. Accessed 26 Feb. 2021.

33. Whittaker and Koo, "Proteus Anguinus."

34. "Red-Eyed Tree Frog." *National Geographic*, n.d., nationalgeographic.com. Accessed 26 Feb. 2021.

35. Mary-Ann Muffoletto. "Fang-tastic: USU Biologist Reports Amphibians with Snake-Like, Venomous Dental Glands." *Utah State University*, 6 July 2020, usu.edu. Accessed 26 Feb. 2021.

36. "Ringed Caecilia." *EOL*, n.d., eol.org. Accessed 26 Feb. 2021.

37. "Toxic Newts." *PBS Learning Media*, n.d., tpt.pbslearningmedia.org. 0:40. Accessed 26 Feb. 2021.

38. "Tomato Frog." *EOL*, n.d., eol.org. Accessed 26 Feb. 2021.

39. Aaron Rudolph. "Dyscophus Antongilii." *Animal Diversity Web*, 2017, animaldiversity.org. Accessed 26 Feb. 2021.

40. "Painting of Wallace's Flying Frog." *Google Arts and Culture*, n.d., artsandculture.google.com. Accessed 26 Feb. 2021.

INDEX

Adriatic Sea, 75
Africa, 39
Amazon rain forest, 20, 23, 47
Asia, 15, 79
Australia, 22–23
Aztec culture, 67

birds, 9–10, 13, 15, 22, 31, 35, 63, 79
breathing, 8, 11, 12, 18, 26, 30, 32, 53, 55, 59, 61, 66, 74, 92

caecilians, 7, 8, 11, 84–87
California, 15, 91
calls, 14, 17, 21, 43, 46–47, 51, 63, 76
Cameroon, 48, 51
camouflage, 18, 51, 79
Canada, 30, 31, 34, 35
cane beetles, 22
captive breeding, 47, 51, 55, 63, 67, 95
captivity, 38, 46, 47, 75
caves, 26, 37, 72–75
Central America, 40, 43, 83
China, 24, 27, 79

Chocó people, 45
chytrid fungus, 11, 15, 38–39
classification of amphibians, 5–7
climate change, 10, 83
Colombia, 44–45, 47, 87
color changing, 73, 82
conservation, 44, 47, 55, 67, 71, 75
Costa Rica, 80

defense strategies, 8, 18, 56, 79, 81–82, 88, 92, 94–95
deforestation, 38, 47, 83

efts, 32–35
eggs, 8–9, 18, 22, 32, 37, 43, 46, 51, 52–53, 59, 77, 82, 98–99
   number laid, 12, 22, 27, 31, 40, 48, 66, 75, 93
   parental care, 27, 31, 40, 41, 46, 48, 52, 68–69, 75, 80–81, 87
endangered species, 24, 47, 51, 55, 67, 75

estivation, 61–62
Europe, 15, 36, 39, 73, 75

fish, 12, 13, 15, 18, 26, 27, 28, 31, 35, 50, 51, 55, 63, 64, 67, 83, 90
Florida, 12, 23, 35
frogs, 6, 7, 8, 9, 39, 48–51, 92–95
   bullfrogs, 11, 12–15
   flying frogs, 96–99
   glass frogs, 40–43
   Paedophryne amauensis, 6
   poison frogs, 11, 44–47, 68–71, 90
   toads, 6, 9, 16–23, 76–79
   tree frogs, 80–83

gills, 9, 12, 26–27, 28, 30, 32, 37, 53–54, 59, 60, 65–66, 73–74, 90

habitat loss, 10, 51, 55, 67, 71, 95
hibernation, 15, 37

invertebrates, 9–10, 13, 15, 18, 19, 22, 23, 26, 27, 28, 31, 35, 36, 39, 43, 45, 46, 47, 50, 51, 55, 62, 71, 72, 75, 79, 82, 83, 87, 88, 90, 91, 95, 99

Lake Xochimilco, 64, 67
larvae (amphibian), 8–9, 14, 27, 29–31, 32–33, 35, 37, 53–55, 59, 63, 65, 75, 79, 89, 99
legal protection, 38, 47, 51
limb regeneration, 64–65
live birth, 9, 37
lungs, 8–9, 12, 26–27, 30, 32, 41, 59, 66, 74, 92

Madagascar, 92–93, 95
Malaysia, 96, 99
mammals, 9, 31, 35, 50, 51, 87
mating, 13–14, 17, 21–22, 26–27, 34, 43, 46–47, 59, 63, 66, 70–71, 75, 76–77, 80–81, 89, 93, 98–99
medical research, 10, 44–45, 65

metamorphosis, 8–9, 12, 14, 22, 27, 32–35, 37, 43, 49–50, 53–55, 59, 65, 75, 83, 93, 99
Mexico, 43, 63, 64–67, 83
mimicry, 69–70
monogamy, 70–71

nest construction, 26–27, 48–49, 52
North America, 13, 15, 19, 23, 91

poaching, 24, 38, 47, 75, 95
poison, 8, 11, 18, 20–23, 35, 44–47, 56, 68–71, 79, 81, 88, 90
pollution, 67, 75, 83, 95

salamanders, 6–7, 36–39, 56–59
  axolotls, 64–67
  giant salamanders, 11, 24–27
  hellbenders, 52–55
  mudpuppies, 28–31
  newts, 32–35, 88–91
  olms, 72–75
  sirens, 60–63

scientists, 4–5, 7, 10, 24, 38–39, 41, 43, 44–45, 49, 51, 52–53, 57, 63, 65, 67, 71, 75, 82, 85, 87, 90, 98
snakes, 10, 13, 18, 31, 45, 56, 63, 82, 85, 87, 88, 90, 92
South America, 15, 23, 43, 71, 84, 87

tadpoles, 12–15, 18, 19, 22, 23, 40, 43, 46, 49–50, 62, 68–69, 81–83
temperature regulation, 8
tongues, 13, 16, 18, 46, 56
toxins, 4, 8, 21, 44–45, 46, 55, 79, 90

United States, 23, 28, 30, 31, 34–35, 55, 59, 63, 91

venom, 30, 85
vision, 6–7, 25, 55, 72, 79

Wallace, Alfred Russel, 98

ABOUT THE AUTHOR
Marie Pearson

Marie Pearson is an author and editor of books for young readers. Her favorite topics are about nature, especially animals. She has always found amphibians fascinating and has a particular fondness for olms. She has an Australian shepherd and standard poodle, whom she enjoys training for a variety of dog sports.

ABOUT THE CONSULTANT
Brian I. Crother, PhD

Brian I. Crother, PhD, is the Schlieder Foundation Professor of Biological Sciences at Southeastern Louisiana University in Hammond. He earned his BS from California State University at Dominguez Hills and his PhD from the University of Miami (FL), and he conducted postdoctoral research at the University of Texas, Austin. He has contributed to well over 100 publications on a broad range of topics, including by editing the books *Caribbean Amphibians and Reptiles* and *Ecology and Evolution in the Tropics: A Herpetological Perspective*. He also was the chair and coauthor of the fifth through eighth editions of the *Scientific and Standard English Names of Amphibians and Reptiles of North America North of Mexico*. He is a former president of the Society for the Study of Amphibians and Reptiles and the American Society of Ichthyologists and Herpetologists. His research interests are broad but largely cover amphibians and reptiles.